Old CALLANDER and the TRO

by
Bernard Byrom

Callander's Dreadnought Hotel (on the left of the picture) was built in 1820 to replace the original Callander Inn which is the white-painted building on its far side. The bow-fronted section nearest to the camera was added in 1891. The hotel was built by the then chieftain of the Clan MacNab, the motto of which is 'Dread Nought'. Its upper section fronting onto Leny Road incorporates a carving of the clan emblem, the severed head of the chief of Clan MacNeish, which was almost entirely wiped out by the MacNabs in the course of a skirmish on Loch Earn in 1612. The building facing it across Leny Road is now the Riverside Inn, but once housed a cinema and the post office.

ACKNOWLEDGEMENTS

Many people have helped in the preparation of this book and it is impossible to name them all. The internet, too, has been a valuable source of information and has also enabled cross-checking of dates and events. In particular, though, I would like to thank Susan Allan and Tom Sherry of the Rob Roy & Trossachs Visitor Centre, Callander, for their help in locating the whereabouts and present-day uses of many of the buildings in and around Callander.

FURTHER READING

So many useful books have been written about the history of the area and its flamboyant personalities that it is impossible to list them all here. The Rob Roy & Trossachs Visitor Centre at Callander and the Visitor Centre at Aberfoyle stock an extensive range of such books and are well worth a visit. In addition, the staff are extremely knowledgeable about the area. Two recent books in particular are recommended reading for an in-depth introduction to the area:

W.F. Hendrie, *The Trossachs History & Guide*, 2004.
P.J.G. Ransom, *Loch Lomond and the Trossachs in History and Legend*, 2004.
Earlier publications include:
The Statistical Accounts of Scotland, 1791–1799 and 1845.
John Thomas, *The Callander & Oban Railway*, 1966, updated by J. Farrington, 1990.
None of these books are available from Stenlake Publishing.

The sign for Duncan's Temperance Hotel is prominent in this picture of Callander which dates from 1918. On the extreme left is a part of the old-established Crown Hotel. In the building beyond it are now Rogerson's shoe shop, the Viewfinder Gallery and, in the second archway, a charity shop.

INTRODUCTION

'The Trosacks are often visited by persons of taste who are desirous of seeing nature in her rudest and most unpolished state.' So wrote the Rev. James Robertson, Minister of Callander, in his entry for the parish in the 1791 *Statistical Account of Scotland*. Many people believe that it was the Victorians who popularised the Trossachs but here we have evidence that they were appreciated as far back as the reign of King George III.

This was the very beginning of the Romantic Age, when people's eyes were being opened to the beauties of nature and places that had hitherto been regarded as wild and barbarous now became regarded in a different light. Although the *Statistical Account* was meant to be just that, the Rev. Robertson took the opportunity to write a glowing 53-page travel guide to the area which would not be out of place in a travel agent's brochure today. His descriptions of the scenic beauties are interspersed with geological observations and philosophical dissertations which make delightful reading. He even manages to include a grammatical guide to the Gaelic language.

Callander is located on the old military road from Stirling to Fort William and stands at an important crossroads where roads from Glasgow, Stirling and Aberfoyle meet. The military roads were built after 1715 by English army engineers to allow troops to move quickly through the Highlands to suppress any local uprisings against King George II.

The oldest part of the town lies south of the bridge over the River Teith at Bridgend. As far back as 1739 plans had been made to develop the north side of the river but these plans received a severe setback when the estates of the Duke of Perth, chief of Clan Drummond and the principal landowner in the district, were forfeited after the 1745 Jacobite rebellion. The Duke's lands were administered for some years by the Commissioners for the Forfeited Estates and in 1763 they began laying out the present wide Main Street and Ancaster Square, specifically for the settlement of army pensioners. The Baronetcy of Callander and a portion of its lands were eventually restored to a branch of the Drummond family in 1784. The parish church was moved in 1773 from its site near Tom na Chessog to a position in the north square which was, at the same time, named Ancaster Square after the Duke of Perth's successor.

The infamous Highland Clearances had an effect as far south as Callander. In the 20 years after 1770 the number of sheep in the area increased from 2,000 to 18,000 and by that time in the village there were two lint mills, four meal mills, one for bruising lint and rapeseed, one fulling mill for woollen cloth, one threshing mill for grain, and there were also three kilns with cast-iron floors for drying grain. By 1798 about a hundred looms were engaged in weaving muslin on the cottage principle at Callander and in the adjoining village of Kilmahog. About a hundred girls also found employment in tambour (embroidery) work. The linen yarn and muslin were bought by Glasgow manufacturers and the woollen yarn by Stirling carpet makers. While the women and girls worked in the textile industry, the men were mainly employed in agricultural labouring.

The Rev. Robertson also mentioned that there was an inn in Callander which was very well kept but he bemoaned the proliferation of ale-houses (or dram-houses) which he described as 'sinks of iniquity which corrupt the morals of the people, ruin their constitutions and squander their subsistence'!

At that time the biggest obstacle to travel was the state of the roads and lack of accommodation. In 1802 the chief of Clan MacNab built a hotel in Callander to house visitors to the area; amongst the tourists who stayed there in 1803 were Wordsworth, Coleridge and Southey, the famous Lakeland Poets.

Callander's rise to prominence as a tourist centre really commenced with the publication in 1810 of Sir Walter Scott's poem 'The Lady of the Lake', which immediately brought a huge influx of visitors to view the beautiful scenery of the nearby Trossachs district which Scott had described. This was followed in 1817 by his historical novel *Rob Roy*, and in 1819 by another novel, *A Legend of Montrose*.

A new hotel was built in 1820, replacing the old Callander Inn of 1802 which stood on the opposite side of the street. The MacNab crest, the bearded head of a chief of Clan MacNeish, was carved above the Leny Road entrance, together with the MacNab motto in Gaelic which translates as 'Dread Nought', hence the name of the hotel.

The coming of the railway to Callander in 1858 marked another important stage in the village's development and in 1866 burgh status was achieved. By the 1880s a number of splendid villas had been erected to the east and west of the town, both for residents and for well-to-do summer visitors who brought with them their entire households, including servants, for the summer 'season'.

It was in 1830 that Thomas Cook first brought a party of tourists through Inversnaid. By 1856 his brochure was stating that a new road had been made between Stronachlachar and Inversnaid and that the new carriages were larger and cheaper to ride in than the old 'drosky'. The coachmen wore scarlet livery and drove four-in-hand carriages.

In 1864 the Prince and Princess of Wales visited the area, sailing from Balloch to Inversnaid. On 4 September 1869 they were followed by Queen

Victoria, who spent an enjoyable holiday staying at Invertrossachs House on the south side of Loch Venachar.

By 1890 there were six four-in-hand coaches a day plying between Callander and the Trossachs. This regular horse-drawn coach service was withdrawn in 1923, and that between Aberfoyle and the Trossachs in 1931, but after the sale of the business the service was retained as a tourist attraction until 1937.

The bed and breakfast era began in the 1930s with the rise in coach tours and private cars. It continued after the Second World War into the 1950s and 60s and was probably at its peak in the 70s. Visitors stayed longer then, but gradually long-stay visits decreased and self-catering and activity holidays became more popular. The tourist steamer service down Loch Lomond to Balloch that used to connect with the coaches lasted until 1989 when the *Countess Fiona* was withdrawn from service. Nowadays, car parks take up large amounts of space and day-visitors and coach tour parties are in the majority.

The other principal village covered by this book is Aberfoyle. In 1791 the Rev. Robert Graham, writing his entry on the parish for the *Statistical Account*, paints a somewhat prosaic picture of his village. He makes no mention of tourism in the area and says that around 1770 almost all the upper part of the parish was converted into sheep farms, for which the soil was very suitable. This was an instance of the Highland Clearances and the population of the parish was considerably diminished as a result. By 1791 several families had moved to Balfron, about eight miles away, where a cotton manufactory was carried on upon an extensive scale.

Bird life abounded in the area. Although black eagles had by then been almost entirely destroyed, ospreys were frequently seen and there were also falcons, waterfowl, ptarmigan and plenty of game birds on the hills. However, by the time of the 1843 *Statistical Account* the minister of that time was reporting that the black eagle and the osprey had both disappeared and the ptarmigan was rarely seen.

In spite of being a relatively healthy area, infant mortality was very high. It was estimated that more than half of children died before they reached ten years of age. In 1791 the population of the parish had been estimated at 790 as against 895 in 1755. Most of the inhabitants of Aberfoyle were farmers or tacksmen; there were a few sub-tenants, shepherds, cottagers and about eighteen handicraftsmen, i.e. smiths, tailors, shoemakers, weavers, shoemakers and carpenters. There were 157 inhabited houses in the village. Gaelic was the language in everyday use but everybody understood English.

By 1843, however, the population of Aberfoyle parish had declined to only 549 and the number of inhabited houses to 130, and this at a time when Callander's prosperity was increasing. It was reported that there was only one inn in the parish which was quite sufficient to supply the needs of both travellers and inhabitants. Clearly something needed to be done to revive the village.

The principal produce of the village was high quality slate but the lack of good transport facilities was a major hindrance to its exploitation. It was not until 1882 that the situation changed, when Aberfoyle was at last connected to the outside world by rail and a tramway was built from near the station up to the slate quarries at the approach to the Duke's Pass. Not only did this enable the slate to be transported cheaply to the expanding towns and cities of Scotland but, at the same time, the Duke of Montrose built a proper coach road, at his own expense, through the pass that now bears his name and over to Loch Katrine.

Hotels were built in the village and at last Aberfoyle could play its proper part in the great Trossachs Tour. Despite losing its railway service in 1951 and the quarries closing in 1958, the development of the tourist industry has meant that this now-prosperous village has never since looked back.

But Callander and Aberfoyle are just two of the many attractions of an area that abounds with history and glorious scenery. Whether the reader is looking for the places that enchanted Queen Victoria or the scenery that inspired Sir Walter Scott to write his epic historical novels about Rob Roy and Montrose, or merely looking for places of beauty and tranquillity, they will find them here.

Opposite: All the buildings in this photograph are still standing but in place of the 1930s confectioners and tearooms selling lunches and teas with Hovis and similar delights, the same shops now comprise a newsagent's shop, followed by the Card Angel Gift Shop, Tartan Treasures, Callander Meadows Restaurant & Gift Shop (in the tall building), Brambles Fashions & Gifts, Callander Woollen Mill, the Threshold Restaurant, the Scotch Oven Tearoom, Sweeties, Tasty Fry Fish & Chips, Nutcrackers Christmas Shop and, finally, Curiosities. On the right-hand side of the street the Dreadnought Hotel is prominent with Blair's Garage (now the car park of a Tesco Express Store) beyond. The mountain behind the village is Ben Ledi, the most southerly of the Highland 'Bens'. The name is a contracted form of *Ben-le-dia*, 'the Hill of God', and it is the most prominent mountain in the district.

C 1123 Main St., Callander.

A cowherd leads a small herd of cattle down Main Street past the old bank building on the right, whilst, in the distance, a shepherd approaches with his flock of sheep taking up most of the roadway. What traffic congestion there would be if this scene were re-enacted today! Blair's garage can be seen beyond the Dreadnought Hotel so the photograph was probably taken sometime in the 1920s or possibly a little earlier. The bank building was built in 1882 for the Commercial Bank which later became the National Commercial Bank. In 1956 the building was bought by the Royal Bank of Scotland. It subsequently became the Sorrisdale Hotel and then the Royal Hotel before being reopened in 2003 as the Old Bank Restaurant. The white building on the right, beyond the bank, is the original Callander Inn, now a shop named Ideas. On the opposite side of the road Geo. McKay's decorating business is now shared between the Sweeties ice cream and the Tasty Fry fish and chip shops, whilst the two cottages beyond are now the Nutcrackers Christmas Shop and Curiosities.

An Edwardian view of Main Street, looking west from Church Street. A modern single-storey building housing Julian Graves's shop has replaced the building on the near left, whilst Duncan's Temperance Hotel later moved to another building across the street and further west. Its old premises were then occupied by the Waverley Hotel which is still in business. Across the street the shop offering genuine reductions in their clearance sale is now the Highland Arts Studio; the small cottages next to it have been demolished and replaced by Mathieson's baker's and Caledonia Countrywear. The shop beyond is currently a café premises that has recently closed for business, whilst the next shop, with the white sunblind, is a branch of Victoria Wine.

Right: This 1920s photograph was taken from Ancaster Square which runs across the picture, the main view ahead being westwards down Main Street. The war memorial is on the left, facing the former parish church, which is out of sight to the right. The building on Main Street with the sign advertising Alex McFarlane's Coal and General Contracting business is now the Main Street Bakery and the door on the left of the sign is the entry to Mariann's Hair Fashions.

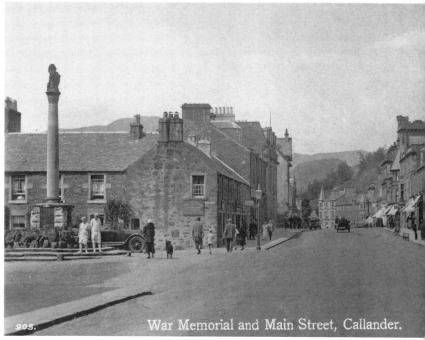

War Memorial and Main Street, Callander.

Left: Ancaster Square is named after the Earl of Ancaster. The date of its creation, 1773, and the initials of its first residents appear above house No. 1. In that year a church was built in the square with a pavilion roof and a spire over the pediment in the front. It was designed by Mr Baxter, architect, and most of the expense was defrayed by the late Commissioners of the Annexed Estates. It was said that the bell in the spire could be heard at a distance of 12 or 14 miles on a 'calm day'. By 1880 the church had become too small to house the growing population of the village and it was decided to build a new one. The present building in the square was constructed in 1883 and was known as Callander Parish Church until 1929 when it was renamed as St Kessog's. Following the union of the church with the former United Free Church of St Bride's in 1985, the latter was used for worship and St Kessog's was converted into the Rob Roy & Trossachs Visitor Centre. A small horse-drawn carriage was waiting patiently in the square when this photograph was taken one afternoon in May 1922. The only shop in sight, Dyet's chemist's shop on the corner, is now James Pringle, weavers.

This 1920s photograph shows the junction of Main Street with Bridge Street (on the left) and Cross Street (on the right). The buildings on the left now contain a newsagent (as in the picture, but under different ownership), the Card Angel Gift Shop, Tartan Treasurers, Callander Meadows Restaurant & Gift Shop (formerly the Callander Inn), Brambles Fashions & Gifts, Callander Woollen Mill, and the Threshold Restaurant. The buildings on the right are now taken by Desirables dress shop, Shell Control, the pharmacy, Jaan Indian restaurant, and Matric betting office (taking up the last two in a newer building where Duncan's Temperance Hotel once stood). The clock on the wall further down the street adorned the Crown Hotel. A group of locals are passing the time of day outside the newsagent's whilst a uniformed chauffeur chats on the opposite corner. The garage sign is hanging from the wall of the Ancaster Hotel on the opposite corner of Cross Street.

CALLANDER

This busy 1950s scene shows the present Dreadnought Hotel on the far left with the original hotel on the opposite corner of Station Road, next to the ornate old bank building. Moving down the street, the 'Bar' sign advertises the Crown Hotel. To its right, the 'Hotel' sign indicates the entrance to Duncan's Temperance Hotel, which occupied the upper floors of the tall building with MacEwan's shop on the ground floor. At this time the pharmacy next door was owned by Boots the Chemists; it has nowadays reverted into private ownership and the traditional pestle and mortar seen earlier have been restored to the front of the building. MacEwan's/Duncan's premises have since been demolished and replaced by a modern building whose architectural style is quite in keeping with the street's architecture. It is occupied by the Matric Betting Office and the Jaan Indian Restaurant. The shop nearest the camera is owned by Shell Control. The other buildings in the street, from Station Road upwards, are Ideas (in the original Dreadnought Hotel), the Old Bank Restaurant, two shops, the Crown Hotel, Rogerson's shoe shop and the Viewfinder Gallery (in the arch below the 'Hotel' sign).

These two hotels stood at the junction of the road from Stirling to Crianlarich (A84) and the road from Glasgow (A81). The photograph was taken around 1930. The hotel on the left was the Ancaster Hotel and the one on the right was the Eagle Temperance Hotel. The ground floor of the Ancaster is now the premises of Nature's Corner Health Foods and Pet Care (its upper floors are empty), whilst the Eagle now houses The Golf Company. The shops next to the former Ancaster Hotel are nowadays the Sandwich Bar, followed by Luckenbooth Scottish Jewellery, a pharmacy, Scoopz Ice Cream and the Callander Knitwear Store.

This very old photograph shows the Dreadnought Hotel before its turreted extension was added onto the far end in 1893, and before the addition of a matching turret on the Station Road corner. Its main entrance was then on Leny Road and was fronted by a substantial stone porch surmounted by two crouching lions. The porch has gone and the stone lions now guard the present-day main entrance in Station Road. The white-painted building at the end of the line of buildings on the right is the original Dreadnought Hotel. Next to it is a house with six windows; the nearest half of the house subsequently had another storey added, the frontage was remodelled and the building became a bank – the present-day Old Bank Restaurant. The white building with the sign above the door was an inn – it is the present Crown Hotel. All the other buildings in the picture are still standing and contain shops. The man in the middle of the road is leaning on his shovel and has a long sweeping brush laid across his wheelbarrow. He was probably employed to keep the streets clear of horse droppings.

Callander Main St., looking East.

Wm. Glen's Ladies' outfitter's shop is prominent in this turn-of-the-century photograph of Main Street looking towards Stirling. The long expanse of Duncan's Temperance Hotel in its original location, with shops occupying the ground floor, can also be seen on the right-hand side of the road, ending with the junction with Church Street. It later became the Waverley Hotel when Duncan's relocated further down Main Street.

British Railways' standard class 4MT 2-6-4 side tank engine, No. 80028, built in 1951, arriving at Callander Station with the two-coach 4 p.m. school train to Crianlarich on 9 September 1965. At this time the line was being run down in preparation for its planned closure two months later. By the time this photograph was taken, the overbridge had already lost its enclosed canopy and clock tower (see the photograph on the following page) and the locomotive has steam leaking from several joints; it isn't even carrying the headlamp code (a single lamp fixed to the bracket below the chimney) that would have denoted it as a stopping passenger train.

The Dunblane, Doune & Callander Railway was first promoted in July 1846 to built a ten-mile line from the Scottish Central line at Dunblane. The scheme was supported by many local men but lapsed due to lack of sufficient financial support. A new Act of Parliament was obtained in 1856 and the line opened on 1 July 1858, with five trains a day in summer and two in winter. From 1 August 1865 the line was absorbed by the Caledonian Railway Company. In 1870 a new company, the Callander & Oban Railway, extended the line as far as Glenoglehead and eventually reached Oban in 1880. The original terminus station in Callander was closed shortly after the Callander & Oban Railway's new station was brought into use in 1870, but it continued in use as a goods and mineral depot until 1965. The site is now covered by a housing development. The new station was built behind the Dreadnought Hotel and was often referred to in railway internal correspondence as the 'Dreadnought' station although it was never publicised as such. It was built on a slight rise behind the town and was backed by a steeply wooded hill. In 1870 a proposed Trossachs Railway was surveyed which would have branched off the Callander & Oban line a mile west of Callander Station and run for just over eight miles along the north shore of Loch Venachar. Nothing came of that, nor of any subsequent proposals to take the railway into the Trossachs. This photograph was taken in 1913.

Callander Station was situated in a spacious area behind the Dreadnought Hotel. It was from here that four-in-hand coaches, laden with happy tourists, and with their drivers resplendent in scarlet coats with shining buttons and white beaver top hats, once departed for the Trossachs. Although this photograph dates from 1950, the station still bears the name of its former owners, the London Midland & Scottish Railway, which had become part of the nationalised British Railways at the beginning of 1948. The station was closed in September 1965 and its site is now a large car and coach park.

Freight services were withdrawn between Callander and Crianlarich (Lower) on 7 September 1964 and passenger services should have followed suit on 1 November 1965 although they were brought to a slightly premature end by a landslide in Glen Ogle on 27 September that year. The rails were quickly ripped up and exported to Mexico where they were used to build the railway between Mexico City and the Olympic Village in time for the 1968 Olympics.

The 'Red Bridge' carries the Aberfoyle road over the Teith to Bridgend. Built in 1908 of red sandstone to replace a picturesque high-arched bridge dating from 1784, it became world-famous through appearing in the opening titles of the television series, Doctor Finlay's Casebook. It was opened in 1908 by Lt-Col. H.E.S. Drummond Hay, Convenor of Perthshire County Council, and Councillor Alex Stock, Provost of Callander. It was paid for partly by local contributions and partly by Perthshire County Council. Salmon, sea trout and brown trout provide good fishing in the river. At one time plentiful supplies of mussels containing fine pearls were to be found in the Teith and brought the villagers considerable profits, but they were exhausted long before Sir Walter Scott made the district famous. The buildings on the right of the picture of Bridgend are now much altered. On the left, the first large house is Ivy Cottage and has a carved stone above the front door depicting a mason's tools. Next to that is another house, then the Bridgend Hotel and, finally, the white house called Teithview.

C 1124 S. Church Street, Callander

Following the 1843 Disruption in the Scottish Presbyterian Church, which saw the establishment of the Free Church, this handsome Free Church building was erected in the village. Its porch bears the date 1907 (probably when the church was rebuilt) but the church hall next door has the inscription of 1849. In 1929 the Free Church and the Established Church made up their differences and united as the Church of Scotland, upon which this church was named St Bride's and the parish church in Ancaster Square became St Kessog's. In 1985 St Kessog's was closed and became the Visitor Centre. All religious services were then held at St Bride's which was renamed Callander Kirk. The sundial still stands at the end of Church Street, although is now protected by a wall.

Sartorial styles may have changed over the years, but very little else has altered on this part of the golf course since this 1930s photograph was taken. Callander Golf Club was formed in 1890 and the first nine holes of its course were designed by the great 'Old' Tom Morris (1821–1908) who had won the Open four times and been runner-up three times, all in the nine years between 1861 and 1869. Old Tom also designed such famous courses as Carnoustie (1867), Royal Dornoch (1887), Muirfield (1891) and the new Course at St Andrews (1894), as well as playing in every Open until 1896 when he was 75 years old. Willie Fernie subsequently designed the back nine holes and Callander Golf Club nowadays boast a Par 66 course of 5,126 yards. At the end of the Seven Years' War in 1763, a soldiers' settlement was established in an area which is now part of the golf course.

A large hydropathic hotel, a typical feature of Victorian 'health' resorts, was built south of the river and lasted until the Second World War. It was owned by the Callander and Trossachs Hydropathic Company Ltd and designed in 1879 by the well-known architectural firm of Peddie & Kinnear, who were also responsible for, among many other public buildings, the great Caledonian Hotel at the west end of Princes Street, Edinburgh. The Hydro burned down in 1891 and was rebuilt, only to burn down again in 1895. It was then rebuilt a second time. This photograph was taken in December 1927. During the Second World War the hotel was taken over by the military who treated it so roughly that it never again opened its doors as a hotel. Following yet another fire it was demolished and the Callander Holiday Park now occupies its site.

The opulent 'Corridor' at the Callander Hydropathic in 1927. In spite of being a health spa, ashtrays abound. There was no such thing as an anti-smoking lobby in those days and smoking was regarded as an essential part of sophisticated life.

TENNIS COURTS, CALLANDER

This view is no more. The railway station was closed in 1965 and is now a car and coach park, whilst the tennis courts have since been replaced by a housing development. The Caledonian Hotel was in the building facing the signal box. It is now the Caledonian House care home.

Roman Camp is a unique country house, the oldest part of which dates from 1625. It was built as a shooting lodge for the Duke of Perth and is set in 20 acres of gardens beside the River Teith. Its name is derived from an adjacent mound near the river, long considered to be a Roman camp but which is, in reality, a deposit left behind by an Ice Age glacier. Reginald Baliol Brett, second Viscount Esher, paid his first visit to Callander in 1893 and fell so much in love with the area that in 1896 he bought the property outright. In the following year he employed the young architect Gerald Dunnage to make additions and alterations. For the most part, he used old materials from the demolition of Acton House and the Manor House at East Standing in Gloucestershire. By 1919 Viscount Esher and his wife regarded Roman Camp as their principal home and it was affectionately referred to as 'Pinkie' from the colour of its harling. This was a colour associated with the Jacobite leanings of its original owners, the Drummonds. This photograph shows the house as it appeared in 1928; Viscount Esher died in 1930 and left the estate to his son Maurice who survived him by only four years. Roman Camp then had to be sold to meet double death duties and was bought by Lady Helen Rae Wilson, wife of Sir James Wilson, baronet of Airdrie, who lived at Invertrossachs House beside Loch Venachar. In 1939 she formed Venachar Hotels Ltd. to run Roman Camp as an exclusive country house hotel. Although in different hands, it is still privately owned and operates as the Roman Camp Country House Hotel.

The mound next to the house comprises a bank enclosing about four acres of ground, the river forming one side, and was formed entirely naturally. In 1791 it was described as being a beautiful waving bank covered with a variety of trees and shrubbery and having a well-dressed terrace on the summit. At that time it was owned by a Captain Fairfoul and was said to have put him in mind of the Bay of Biscay! Nowadays, it is more overgrown than in the photograph but still makes a pleasant walk.

Richard Hill sold groceries but the greater part of his shop was given over to his business in wines and spirits. The shop was situated where the licensed Dalgair House Hotel now stands so it has not entirely changed its function. Although now Reid's Restaurant, the shop frontage is unchanged.

Another old-established Callander business that has stood the test of time. This photograph from around 1900 shows the apothecary's shop at No. 27 Main Street with its traditional pestle and mortar symbol above the door and a sign advertising Kodak photographic materials. Nowadays the shop is called the Trossachs Pharmacy and its entrance has been moved to the middle of the frontage, which has itself been modernised. In all other respects its appearance is still the same as it was over a hundred years ago and the elaborate doorway on the left is totally unchanged.

Opposite: Loch Venachar is four miles long and, while its deepest point is 111 feet, the average depth is only 42 feet. There are lots of trout and pike in the loch, although the latter tend to frighten away other types of fish. The River Teith emerges from the eastern end of the loch and joins the River Leny at Callander. The south shore is covered by woodlands which contain a maze of forest tracks and pathways. The loch begins only a mile west of Callander and has been described as 'a little haven of peace and quiet'. A pebble beach is exposed when the water level is low and interesting rock samples can sometimes be found. This boating party, photographed in the summer of 1904, was preparing to hoist sail, possibly for a day's fishing or maybe just for a quiet sail up the loch. The gentleman on the right seems more interested in the pebbles, or has he just dropped his watch? The mansion of Invertrossachs, which was visited by Queen Victoria in 1869, stands on the loch's southern shore. The building has been extensively extended and modernised since then, but most of the original building has survived and now provides bed and breakfast and self-catering accommodation.

This tranquil scene is now the busy A84 westwards out of Callander. It was in this area, known as the Leny Feus, that many large villas were built in Victorian times to accommodate well-to-do families on their summer holidays. Many of these families would not only spend the entire summer here, but would bring their domestic servants as well. The amount of luggage they brought was mountainous, hence the need for such spacious platforms as existed at Stirling, Perth and Callander railway stations.

Kilmahog is a hamlet situated on the River Leny a mile to the west of Callander at the junction of the Trossachs and Lochearnhead roads. It derives its name from 'Cell of St Chug' and was an early ecclesiastical centre. In 1791 there were about 48 families. They had long leases which encouraged them to build better quality houses. The village is the junction for the scenic routes leading to the Trossachs by way of Lochs Venachar and Achray and to the Central Highlands via the Pass of Leny. The artist John Everett Millais and John Ruskin stayed in the village for four months in 1853 and William and Dorothy Wordsworth also paid it a visit. There is a preserved eighteenth century woollen mill which nowadays offers Highland dress, tartans, kilts and a large selection of Aran, cashmere and lambswool knitwear. This view, probably from the 1920s, is looking up the main road from Callander towards Lochearnhead. The house on the right is the former tollhouse and the road from Aberfoyle and the Trossachs joins from the left. In earlier days the bay window enabled the toll-keeper to keep a watchful eye on traffic approaching from every direction.

The Wayside Tearoom stood on the left-hand side of the road to Aberfoyle just after it leaves the A84 Callander road at Kilmahog. It was extensively remodelled and more than doubled in size over forty years ago when it was upgraded into the Lade Inn which is still in business. The old building can still be recognised as the central part of the inn. It stands on the site of a former mill which was powered by a lade which ran from the nearby River Leny.

This view of the old bridge at Gartchonzie is looking north towards the modern road from Callander to the Trossachs. The bridge was built around 1777. In the foreground the road to the left runs along the south side of Loch Venachar and leads towards Invertrossachs House where Queen Victoria stayed on her visit to the area in 1869. To the right of the bridge the road leads to Bridgend and the centre of Callander.

Brig o' Turk derives its name from the Gaelic for 'Wild Boar', which is probably a reference to early porcine inhabitants who once roamed the area. Queen Victoria stopped at the original Brig o' Turk Inn in 1869 because she wished to meet 'Muckle Kate', the landlady who, at 25 stone, was reputed to be the largest woman in the United Kingdom. They enjoyed a chat together and, on leaving, the Queen presented Kate with two golden sovereigns. These became Kate's most prized possessions, but she didn't enjoy them for long because she died only three years later. Just to the left of the roadside after the bend are the village's famous tearooms. Nowadays, Brig o' Turk is a small, scattered village whose inhabitants, besides a fair sprinkling of commuters, also include those employed in the forestry, water and tourism industries.

Tea Room, Brig o'Turk.

This tearoom is almost an institution. Whilst it has been in business for years, and is extremely popular with cyclists and walkers, its outward appearance is unchanged from this 1930s photograph. It stands at the foot of the road up to the Glen Finglas reservoir which, when it was completed in 1965, submerged the hamlets of Duart and Achnahard.

BRIG O'TURK, CALLANDER

This old bridge carries the A821 road from Loch Katrine across the River Turk at the western approach to the village. The photograph was taken in the summer of 1910 when the waters were running very low and the elegant lady was able to walk almost to the middle of the river without getting her feet wet.

The McGregor family proudly pose with their new motorcar outside their cottage at Strathgarthney in the 1920s. The house has since been enlarged by the addition of a conservatory at one end and a stone extension at the other, but is still easily recognisable today. One thing that has changed, however, is the roadway – it was in far better condition 80 years ago!

Post Office, Brig o'Turk.

D. McAdam's motor business and post office stood on the main road through Brig o' Turk on the opposite side from the famous tearoom just down the road. The building still stands but is now the Burnt Inn House hotel, whilst the post office has relocated to a newer building nearby. The old petrol pump may have gone, but the building, although enlarged, is easily recognisable as the former garage.

In the 1820s a farmhouse on the north side of Loch Arklet known as Archeanochrochan was converted into a public house and then into an inn to cater for the large number of visitors attracted to the area by Sir Walter Scott's novels. It was replaced around 1850 by the construction of the Trossachs Hotel, built in Scottish baronial style. The hotel was extended in 1877 and again in 1891, when additional wings were added. In this picture two young men are relaxing in the field between the hotel and Loch Arklet; the one on the right appears to be sketching the view across the loch towards Ben Lomond. Nowadays, greatly enlarged and extended from the original hotel shown here, it is a luxurious timeshare complex named *An Tigh Mor*, Trossachs (literally 'The Big House').

This late-Victorian photograph shows four coaches loaded with tourists who had recently arrived from Stronachlachar on the then newly built *Sir Walter Scott*, the funnel of which can be seen in the middle distance. The scene is still easily recognisable today, but the area is now marked out with car parking bays and the tearooms on the right have become the modern Captain's Rest licensed refreshment rooms. For centuries Loch Katrine was MacGregor country, whose clansmen stole cattle from the Lowlands and tussled with the authorities. Not for nothing were they known as the 'Children of the Mist'. In more recent times Loch Katrine was immortalised by Sir Walter Scott but some of the locations featured in his writings have disappeared beneath the water (see pages 38 and 40). The Silver Strand, a beach of white quartz pebbles, completely disappeared; Ellen's Isle was reduced in size and the whole shape of the loch was changed forever by the rising waters. The name 'The Trossachs', meaning 'The Bristly Country', properly applies only to the short rocky pass between Loch Achray and Loch Katrine, but nowadays it covers a much wider area. The pass through the Trossachs between Aberfoyle and Loch Katrine is called 'The Duke's Pass' after the Duke of Montrose who built it in 1855. Prior to that, only a packhorse track went over these hills.

The interior of the old tearooms at Loch Katrine Pier with springtime flowers decorating the tables. The notice on the wall in Gaelic, *Ceud Mile Failte*, is an old Scottish toast and can be translated into English as 'A Hundred Thousand Welcomes'. The tearooms have been updated into the present-day Captain's Rest licensed refreshment rooms.

The *Sir Walter Scott* raises steam at Loch Katrine Pier, ready to take on passengers for its journey down the loch to Stronachlachar. This steamer, launched in 1899, is the fifth boat and fourth steamer to ply the loch. Before the days of steam power, travellers were conveyed by the *Water Witch*, a rowing boat with an eight-man crew. For this, there was one run up and down the loch each day: passengers disembarked at Coalbarns near Stronachlachar and either walked or rode to Inversnaid whilst the boatmen carried their luggage. Ponies were on hand to convey ladies, the elderly and infirm along the rough track, but the others had to walk. On wet days that was bad enough but the Highland ghillies often levied blackmail (i.e. requests for 'gratuities' if they were to complete the journey safely), just as their ancestors had done to guarantee the protection of farmers' cattle. In 1843 the Loch Katrine Steamboat Company launched the paddle steamer *Gypsy*, the first steamship on the loch. She had been transported there from Callander, the ten-mile journey having taken eleven days. However, she had not been in service longer than about a week before she was sunk in mysterious circumstances, suspicion falling on the redundant oarsmen from the *Water Witch*. However, the crew of the *Water Witch* resumed the service but two years later the steamship company tried again with another paddle steamer, *Rob Roy*, which operated for several years before being sold to the contractor for Glasgow Waterworks. Her successor, which in the picture is moored in the inlet just beyond the *Sir Walter Scott*, was the screw-propelled *Rob Roy II* which was launched in 1855 and conveyed Queen Victoria when she opened Loch Katrine reservoir in 1859. When the *Sir Walter Scott* was launched in 1899, the two boats operated the service together for a year before *Rob Roy II* was laid up in the inlet; it never returned into service.

The reflections in the still waters of the loch in this Victorian photograph, taken around 1870, are so clear that it could very easily be published upside down! Since this time the level of the loch has been raised by several feet to provide greater reserves of water for the citizens of Glasgow. The thatched boathouse with five rowing boats lined up by the waters edge is now a souvenir shop and the expanse behind it is now marked out as a car and coach park.

The *Sir Walter Scott* was built by William Denny of Dumbarton in 1899 at a cost of £4,250, and was loaded onto barges which took her to Inversnaid by way of the River Leven and Loch Lomond. She was then taken overland on horse-drawn carts up the very steep hill out of Inversnaid to Stronachlachar, where she was assembled and launched. She is 110 feet in length, 19 feet wide, weighs 115 tons, and is the only screw-driven steamer on a regular (summer only) passenger service in Scotland. When launched she was licensed to carry 416 passengers, but this has since been reduced to 320. Being fired with (relatively) smokeless solid fuel, she does not contaminate the waters of the reservoir with diesel fuel and her bilge water is dealt with ashore. In 1954 the West of Scotland Water Authority took over the Loch Katrine Steamboat Company in order to exercise stricter control over the quality of the water in the loch, and they are the current owners of the vessel.

As you approach Stronachlachar by road a private track to the south leads to Royal Cottage. Loch Katrine is the largest of the reservoirs that supply Glasgow with its water. It was way back in 1855 that an Act of Parliament was passed which resulted in the level of the loch being raised by four feet and allowed an aqueduct 26 miles long, with a fall of only 10 inches per mile, to be constructed to Milngavie on the north side of Glasgow. The Royal Cottage was built on the shore of Loch Katrine, next to the reservoir's outlet to the aqueduct, especially to house Queen Victoria when she opened the project there on 14 October 1859. The weather was atrocious that day; the Queen and Prince Albert lunched at the cottage but never stayed there! Now greatly changed in its appearance, it is owned by Scottish Water and used by their personnel. Further Acts of Parliament in 1885 and 1919 allowed the level of the loch to be raised still higher and, in 1895, a second aqueduct was constructed to Milngavie. Both aqueducts are still in use today. At around 17 feet higher than its original level, the loch nowadays presents a different appearance to what its early Victorian visitors saw.

Stronachlachar, which means 'the mason's point', nowadays consists of a few scattered houses which provide a base for water authority workers. When Dorothy Wordsworth, accompanied by her brother William and Samuel Taylor Coleridge, arrived here on foot from Inversnaid 1803, the loch seemed to Dorothy 'but a dreary prospect – like a barren Ullswater'. There were no boats available for hire, no accommodation to be had and William had to ask for beds for the night at a house near the head of the loch. The village owes its existence to the establishment of the steamer service on Loch Katrine in 1843. The area had become very popular with tourists following the publication in 1810 of Sir Walter Scott's poem, 'The Lady of the Lake', followed by his adventure novel, *Rob Roy*. Early tourists were rowed down the loch by boatmen but this service could not cope with the influx of visitors and so a steamer service was inaugurated. In the summer months steamers would arrive at Stronachlachar packed with tourists and it was quite common to see five or six four-in-hand coaches in procession on the road over the hill to Inversnaid. This picture shows a number of these coaches awaiting the arrival of the steamer from the south end of the loch. The post office and shop in this Victorian building were closed many years ago and have been replaced by a postbox and a soft-drinks vending machine. The almost-bare promontory in the middle background is nowadays completely covered with tall trees planted by the Forestry Commission.

The famous Tour No. 1 began as early as 1859. This was a marathon day excursion by rail and steamship in which the tourist travelled from Glasgow to Balloch by train, Balloch to Inversnaid by steamer, Inversnaid to Stronachlachar by horse-drawn carriage, down Loch Katrine by steamer to the Trossachs Pier, to Callander by carriage, and thence back to Glasgow by train. It proved so successful that it also began to run in the reverse direction as Tour No. 2. This 1934 photograph shows coaches waiting at Stronachlachar for the arrival of the *Sir Walter Scott* from Loch Katrine Pier. Four-in-hand coaches had four rows of seats exclusively for passengers, plus a leading seat where the coachman sat and other passengers could sit with him. There was comfortable seating for around fourteen passengers but, at a pinch, up to twenty passengers could be squeezed on board. This was no joke for the horses as they plodded up the steep winding road from Inversnaid to the top of the hill near the old Garrison Fort. Passengers had to mount the coaches using ladders with eight steps and no handrails. Many of the coaches themselves didn't have rails at the end of the seats and passengers just had to hold on!

The former Stronachlacher Hotel can be seen a short distance west of the present-day pier. Horse-drawn coaches once departed from it for Inversnaid, but it was closed many years ago, before the outbreak of the Second World War. It later became a hostel for Water Authority workers but today it is disused and semi-derelict. Steps ran down from the hotel entrance to the landing stage for the convenience of hotel guests. Travellers joining from road coaches walked down the sloping track leading in from the left of the picture. In this picture the *Sir Walter Scott* is getting up steam in preparation for leaving for the south end of the loch with a fair-sized complement of passengers. The original hotel had been built further round the bay in 1851/2 but was replaced by this building after 1886 due to the level of the loch being significantly raised by an extension of the reservoir project in 1886.

This 1870 photograph shows the *Rob Roy II* landing passengers at the old pier at Stronachlachar, in front of the original hotel, where they are boarding four-in-hand coaches. Launched in 1855, the *Rob Roy II* was taken out of service in 1900, a year after the *Sir Walter Scott* began operating on the loch.

This picture shows a party of American tourists en route from Stronachlachar Pier to Inversnaid in August 1930. Inversnaid is a hamlet with a well-known hotel, situated on the eastern shore of Loch Lomond with spectacular views westwards towards Arrochar. It is linked by road to Stronachlachar on Loch Katrine. It was not until 1959 that the road between Stronachlachar and Inversnaid was taken over by the local authority. Rob Roy MacGregor acquired land at Inversnaid and a barracks was built to the east of the hamlet in 1719 at the request of the Duke of Montrose to defend his territories against Rob Roy as well as to control the Jacobite districts after the 1715 rebellion. The soldiers were withdrawn around 1789 and the building was last occupied around 1796; the buildings became ruinous and are now incorporated into Garrison Farm. Sir Walter Scott passed this way in both 1792 and again in 1828. Visitors in 1803 included William Wordsworth with his sister Dorothy and their companion, Samuel Taylor Coleridge. It was on this visit that William was inspired to write his poem, 'To a Highland Girl'. Jules Verne visited the area in 1859 and was so fascinated by its wildness that in 1887 he wrote a novel, *Les Indies Noire* ('The Black Indies', recently translated into English as *The Underground City*), about an imaginary Utopian community of miners who live in Coal City beneath the waters of Loch Katrine. The hotel at Inversnaid has been greatly enlarged over the years and now does a thriving business with coach tour companies. A passenger foot ferry still connects it with the hamlet of Inverglas on the opposite shore of Loch Lomond and there are wonderful views of the 'Arrochar Alps' from its windows.

Owned by the Aberfoyle Slate Quarry Co. Ltd., these slate quarries date from the eighteenth century and by Victorian times were the third largest in Scotland. There were several in the Aberfoyle area, all producing high quality slates. This quarry is at the side of the Trossachs Road, at the approach to the Duke's Pass travelling north from Aberfoyle. The sturdily built workmen's cottages are all roofed with slate, as is the Quarry Manager's house on the right. A narrow gauge tramway used to connect this quarry with the railway at Aberfoyle. The tramway was closed in 1947 and the quarries themselves closed in 1958. The workmen's cottages have long since been demolished but the Quarry Manager's house still stands at the roadside and is now a holiday cottage.

In the foreground the road to Loch Katrine over the Duke's Pass bends sharply as it climbs steeply away from the village, which is nestling in the bottom of the valley. In the distance the road eastwards to Thornhill and Stirling snakes along the valley. The photograph was taken in the autumn of 1927 and the area is considerably more built-up nowadays.

A panoramic view of Aberfoyle in 1929 with the Bank of Scotland prominent in the centre of the picture and the ivy-clad Bailie Nicol Jarvie Hotel to the left. Stone Age settlers were the first visitors to the Aberfoyle area, followed by the Celts who were the first people to use iron. The first real settlement of Aberfoyle came about because it was situated on the drove road from the North to Falkirk market. In olden days the Grahams, Earls of Mentieth, owned all the land in the parish, but with the failure of the male line, their estate came to the family of Montrose. Around 1760 an estimate was done under the direction of Lord Cathcart for making the upper Forth navigable for small vessels. The intention was that coal would be brought from Bannockburn and manufactories could be established at Aberfoyle which would also export slate. The canal would have ended at Loch Lomond, from where boats would have reached the Clyde via the River Leven. Unfortunately, nothing came of this ambitious scheme, probably because it would have cost too much. The carriage road over the Duke's Pass from the Trossachs to Aberfoyle, which can be seen descending the hill from the left and is marked by a white railing, was completed in 1882 by the Duke of Montrose, possibly to coincide with the opening of the railway to Aberfoyle. Until that time the road had been little more than a scenic path. For many years the new road was a private toll road upon which motors were not permitted, but it was eventually improved and freed from tolls in the 1930s.

The building on the corner is now occupied by the Bank of Scotland. Next to it is a restaurant that has recently closed down. Then comes a doorway marked 'Trossachsbank' which gives access to apartments above the shops. Beyond it is a coffee shop and then the post office. The fine building next to it with a turret has been demolished and replaced with a single-storey shop housing the Scottish Co-op but the next building with two gables still survives, being the A2Z gift shop and the Town House Hotel. The garden beyond it has been replaced by a new building housing the police station and the Old Curiosity Shop antiques and bric-a-brac shop. The furthest building is now the World of Football and the Mill Shop. The biggest changes have occurred across the road where the open space is now occupied by two new buildings built on the site of the old railway station. These are the Guyana Garden Centre and Gift Shop (taking the position nearest the camera), with the Forth Inn situated beyond it.